"Don't Tread on Me"
The Fight over Gun Rights is about America's Core Constitutional Freedoms

T. H. Logwood

" A well regulated Militia, being necessary to the security of a free State, the right of the people to keep and bear Arms, shall not be infringed. _2nd Amendment to the US Constitution"

Introduction - History Will Repeat Itself

There was yet another shooting, another gunman trying to murder as many innocent and defenseless people as possible, and the media (and politicians) cry out for more gun control. These events are horrible and tragic in every sense, and all us should bereave the loss of our fellow citizens. It is so tragic that in Our great country, these terrible actions occur. Let us all lift up those effected in prayer, and work together to bring healing and unity in the aftermath.

But more gun control? Will more laws solve the issue? The politicians come up with a myriad of crazy solutions, but continue to ignore the problem. There are plenty of gun laws on the books, good ones, but they are not fully enforced. Add a thousand more laws and regulations, yet it will do nothing more than keep good honest citizens from legally being able to protect themselves. On the other hand, criminals and illegal aliens are armed with all sorts of firearms, laws or not.

It is telling how the media, the Hollywood elites, and various politicians, don't as much greave with the victims of such shootings (as President Trump does), but instead just cry out for more controls and confiscation. These clamorous groups demand intensive Universal background checks, limits on magazine size, eliminating certain types of weapons from the marketplace, are their typical knee-jerk emotional reactions. There is increased talk about gun confiscation, which has made its way into the rhetoric of various political campaigns. They often cite countries like Australia, and how banning guns has "worked" there. Just taking away guns will solve the problem of gun violence and crime? Are these the answers?

No! "Guns don't kill people, people kill people." Gun restricting laws do not save lives, but actually puts more people at risk. Restrict the good and regular law-abiding citizen from protecting themselves, and only the criminals and government will have guns. Does that make us safer? In America, certain areas have high crime rates, other areas are less so, and the loss of life must never be down played. Life is precious, everyone's, not just one group or another, but everybody. All the laws in the world can never end gun violence. Why? Because criminals don't obey laws, it is that simple.

Honest citizens follow the law, and adding more gun restrictions just hurts everyone. The bigger picture is simply this, the federal government does Not have the constitutional right to restrict or regulate our firearms. Yet, our rights as private citizens are greatly restricted by many federal, state, and local laws. If the founding Fathers could only see how much we have shredded our county's establishment, they would call for another revolution. These are perilous times, and sadly, with every disastrous or tragic event, "We the People" eagerly surrender more and more of our freedoms to the central government.

The 2nd Amendment reads: "A well regulated Militia, being necessary to the security of a free State, the right of the people to keep and bear Arms, shall not be infringed".

What that means is that the feds are to "piss off" (according to one commentator), regarding any regulation of our firearms. Study the history and the intent of the founding Fathers when they wrote the Bill of Rights. They had a great document for establishing the new country, but they felt something more was needed to define individual Rights that the federal government should not touch. Everything else not specifically stated was to be relegated to the States. The whole point of the revolution was that the central government was unjust and "tyrannical" in the abuse of governing powers towards the citizens. It was only because the citizens had arms, and took up arms, to defy the government, that there was a revolt. Without the governed having their firearms, the government would have simply used their armaments and force to squash any opposition. In fact, they tried, but the people fought back. And they will do so again, even our very own elected government.

The government, the federal government at least, is not to limit or restrict this right. It is most closely related to the 1st Amendment of free speech because the people have the right to speak out against the government, and to assemble (peacefully). Also the 2nd is closely associated with the 4th and 5th, as the people have the rights to own property and not be subject to search and seizure without due process. The more you read and learn about those early days of the nation and the development of the constitution, the more is explained as to the ideas what the government should not have control over.

At the end of this book, all 27 Amendments are listed for your reference and further study.

The point of this book is to alert and remind ourselves that we are a nation of laws, and they are implemented by "due process". And that we as citizens have rights and freedoms guaranteed to us by our founding document, the Constitution. But all of these rights are greatly under siege by groups and politicians seeking to restrict and remove every freedom we hold dear, certainly pertaining to our rights to own and bear arms.

Rather than get into the "nuts and bolts" of the laws and proposed ideas of what and how new and old regulations work, my intent is to suggest that our "inalienable rights" are being squashed. We, as a free people, need to educate ourselves, and determine for ourselves where and which way we want our governing leaders to guide us. It is through the power of your vote, which is your voice, to elect those leaders that uphold your values and traditions. There are a number of ideas and topics discussed that will hopefully inspire you to learn more, and inspire you to do something (at least vote).

There was a humorous but pointed story that is greatly appropriate. "A bunch of sheep were happily grazing in the field, enjoying the comforts of their lives. A wolf came out of the woods and killed one of the sheep. In a panic, they formed a consensus on what to do. They decided the best way to keep themselves safe was to remove all of their teeth. Later, the wolf came back and killed them all." Get the picture? This is the push the leftists, the media, and the weak-kneed limp-wristed politicians are screaming for. Are we better off disarmed, or have some means to protect ourselves?

The Right to Fight

The modern day fight over Gun Rights is Not about having a few hunting rifles or shotguns. It is about the people being able to defend themselves, and, stand up against the federal government with a counter-force, when said government becomes "tyrannical." Gun rights is also about the Rights of the people to have and own personal property (the 4th Amendment), the Rights of Free Speech, Worship, and to assemble, openly criticize the government (1st Amendment), plus the others set forth in the original Bill of Rights. But it is the 2nd that really defends the others. It was made the second for a reason, it's important. Remember, our forefathers went through a long struggle with a governing body that prompted the whole revolt. They put together the best and most fair principles in establishing and running a country as ever has been written, with "the people" in mind.

According to a news story, America ranks about 53rd in the world for gun violence. However, to the slanderous "fake-news" media, America is the "only" country where guns kill people. Not true, not even close to being realistic at all. And every country has murder and assault crimes without guns, like stabbings, poisonings, and so on. To say that America is riddled with gun violence is totally misstated, yet mainstream media pushes a different narrative. It is no less a horrid part of our culture or human existence, but learn the facts. And factually put, guns stop a great many would-be crimes, but that is never talked about in the media or anti-gun groups. Do your own research and learn for yourselves what is true and accurate.

The larger cities have higher rates of violent crime, and those involving guns than rural areas with lower densities of people, obviously. Too often and in high proportions of the events, it is gang shootings, drugs and other crime related activities, illegal aliens involved in criminal actions, where most gun violence occurs. These criminals do not care about what laws are out there, what weapon bans are in place, they will get the weaponry that they want. Again, do your research and learn who and where gun violence actually occurs. Go talk with your local law enforcement, search for crime stats at the FBI website, there is a lot of sources for information out there. My intent is not to cite stats, but to incite discussion and questions for you to follow up on.

George Floyd - Gun Rights Under Attack

The point of the Second Amendment is, that people have the legal right to have guns (or other arms) for their self-defense, protection of their property (namely the home) , and family. Also, if the government gets too out of control, the people should be able to rise up and overthrow them (by force if needed). And, government is not to enact any laws that interfere or limit this right. What has happened?

But every few days there seems to be yet another tragedy involving guns. Whether right or wrong, the whole issue is highly emotional for some, which then obscures the facts or reality. The underlying issue is that those left wing activist groups shout for ever more gun control and total confiscation, versus our Right to keep and bear arms. It is powder keg that can very truly start another civil war.

Among the latest event, was yet another police brutality story resulting in the death of a black man. This time, it was a policeman in Minneapolis, Minnesota, not a shooting, but the incident resulted in the death of a young black man named George Floyd. The circumstances were tragic, but the result had been a wild flurry of angry mob riots and protests, not just in the city of Minneapolis where the incident took place, but nearly nationwide. And with that, the mobs went crazy, and the media and politicians cry out for more gun control, and with ever more animosity towards the police.

This particular event was horrible and tragic in every sense, and all us should bereave the loss of the victim. It is so tragic that in Our great country, these terrible actions occur, but they do. We have a free and open society, where wrongs will be made, but we have hope in our justice and electoral system will make things right and fair. For even a single moment, can we come together and lift up those effected in prayer? Can we strive to work together to bring healing and unity in the aftermath?

Apparently not. But more gun control? Will more laws solve the issue? In the aftermath of the George Floyd, the rift between those wanting law and order, versus those without any morale compass. It is more than a gun control issue, but guns are a part of the picture. We must have laws, and those people willing to defend and enforce the laws (like policemen with firearms). Otherwise, society breaks down into anarchy, where only the strong dictate the rules (and they do have guns). If these lawless bands can dictate to the politicians to defund (essentially disarm) the police that are suppose to protect us, then that defies many of our cherished rights, does it not? Where would fairness or justice be then? Mob rule, by force, and by what standards or edicts, "the law of the jungle"?

Without rehashing the details of the Floyd case, like the major media had done over and over for weeks, the matter is another sign that civil unrest is a powder keg in the gun control issue. Some refer to this case as police brutality, others cite racial prejudice and "white supremacy". Both sides may have merit, but if even of these criminals (and politicians) really cared about Mr. Floyd, police brutality, rights, or gun control, violence and riots is not the right way to push an a position.

The news media have shewed the truth of the incident, but basically what happened was a black man got into a confrontation with a police officer, and the officer used excessive force that killed the civilian. The particular force used was unwarranted according to the news media, lawyers, and the general public. The officer was subsequently charged with murder. This was despite the fact that the man was a former felon, with evidence of narcotics in his system, and that the struggle was something the officer had to do for his own protection. This was both a horrible and tragic situation, and no one ever wants this to happen.

But the result has been civil unrest and violence not seen for a few years, and has spurred on the controversy of the police, racism, and guns (in the hands of police). Violent protests and riots, destroying private property of individuals and businesses, along with physical violence against innocent people, then sprang up in many major cities for weeks. How much of this was for the wrongful death of

Mr. Floyd? If these people really cared about Mr. Floyd, would they not be peaceful and melancholy?

Unnecessary police brutality in this case is one thing, but then this incident again brought up the whole controversy of police versus black people. The criminal groups of Black Lives Matter and Antifa, and perhaps others, were "allowed" to rampage through the streets of Minneapolis, looting and destroying property without consequence. The new demands by the riotous mobs were to "defund" the various police departments, which are suppose to protect lives and property from violence. Other cities also had protest marches, with rioting taking place in some of these.

Interesting to note, this prompted a case of illegal gun seizure occurred during the Floyd riots. As riots and protests were happening in many cities, in Saint Louis, Missouri, had an incident that should raise an unsettling :red flag". In Saint Louis, the peaceful protests quickly turned into a violent riot, with destruction of private property, businesses being looted, fires, and attacks on innocent people. The mob was then headed towards the mayor's home, on a private (not public) road, inside a private community, with iron gates.

The rioters broke down the gate, and were headed towards the mayors home, hurling objects (such as rocks), yelling and shouting, as they moved along. As they approached the McCluskey's home, the couple moved onto their porch with firearms. They called 911, but help from the police never came. Mr. McCluskey had a rifle (of some sort), and his wife had an (unloaded) pistol. Nothing happened as the rioters moved away, but several days later, the police showed up and confiscated their firearms, and the district attorney, Kim Gardner, charged the couple with some type of assault charge (a felony). Rather than stop the rioters or charge any of them for the crimes they blantanly committed, this democrat attorney went after the would-be victims.

Was that legal? Was it right or fair? There was the potential of violence, personal harm, theft, and destruction of their private home, by rioting criminals, yet the McCluskey's were charged a felony?

Can you not defend your home, property, or even your person, from the potential of harm? And without having the police show up to defend you, you better have your own means

Now the McCluskey's as it was told, are civil right attorney's, which a strange irony to this civil rights like situation. What rights do they, or anyone have in such an event? At least in Missouri, there is the Castle Doctrine, the Stand Your Ground Law, and a law concerning brandishing a weapon. As the case gets national attention and eventually settled, the issue is one that greatly threatens everything the constitution is suppose to guarantee at its core. The rights to own property (home, car, and stuff), defend yourself (and family) from potential harm, and the ownership and use firearms to back up those rights, are exactly the whole point. We are suppose to have rights, unless politically motivated (too often democrat politicians) deem otherwise. This is real, research this yourself.

Essentially, if someone in public authority (like the district attorney in this case), can deny your inalienable rights, then do you really even have them at all? What does it take for any public or elected official to take your property (like your means of self defense) by some local ordinance, or broader law? What about if someone (like a neighbor or ex-spouse, co-worker, or whoever) says that "so and so" is a threatening person, and the police crash in and take away their guns? As simplistic and far fetched as that may sound, basically that is what the Red Flag laws allows the government to do.

The McCluskey case is different, in that it was local laws and the local attorney that initiated the seizure, but the idea of confiscation via the government, "under the law", is rather unsettling. The anti-gun advocates don't need to get rid of the Second Amendment, they just need to nullify it with laws and regulations. There are more and more cases where firearms are being confiscated via various laws, some rightfully so, but it denotes a frightening trend.

Shortly after the Floyd incident, another black man was shot and killed in Atlanta, Georgia by a policeman. Here too, there was a struggle between the police officer and the man, resulting in the officer shooting and killing him. This added more fuel to the current mayhem, and prompted an armed takeover of a portion of downtown Seattle, Washington.

A mob of rioters took control of about six city blocks of downtown Seattle, Washington for several weeks. It was not a peaceful protest of the Floyd brutality issue, but was a violent mob takeover. They erected barriers to block entrance into the area, businesses and property were destroyed and looted, people shot and injured, plus other crimes. One known celebrity handed out guns. The (democrat) mayor and governor stood by and took no action to end the violence, and the media applauded the "festival" as a peaceful fun-loving event. That is exactly the point, that laws have no effect on criminals acquiring and using firearms for their own gain. And (democrat) politicans will do nothing to halt it.

And these violent riots were not limited to Minneapolis and Seattle, other cities saw similar lawlessness and total disregard for the law. If our governing officials will not protect the citizens, via the laws and rights enshrined, then they want more gun laws to do what? What can new laws do that criminals will abide by? If the government is there to protect the people from gun violence and crime, yet do nothing realistic to fix it, then they must be removed from office. To oust the government, we the people, must vote. Voting is our best method of fixing the problems in our society. America was founded on the principles of law and a due process, and the vote is the mechanism that peaceful change can come about. And the vote then empowers new leadership to enact laws and take actions that will protect the people and our rights.

That is how our system of governing is suppose to work. Leaders are elected by the free-will of the people, to enforce the laws, for the good of society. Now in these situations where the mob has ruled that we the people should not have police departments, or property rights, or personal protection from violence, does that make any sense? Who will protect you? Like in the old west times, you had firearms, and you took care of yourself.

Is closing police departments a service to the people, ending the inherent den of racism prevalent in law enforcement? Or does that just keep firearms out of the people that will defend against lawlessness? The elected officials in these cities, like Minneapolis, Seattle, Washington DC, Baltimore, Atlanta, and others, are acting upon the whims of the mob, versus serving the needs of those who elected them. In every case of violence and shootings of police and black men, over the past many years, has been in cities controlled by democrat leaders. These are some of the same advocates for stricter gun regulations. Do the research to see for yourself.

Anarchy and mob rule violates our Rights of free speech, happiness, the ownership of property (including the shirt on your back), and the ability to pursue a peaceful and safe productive life. "The strong thrive, and the weak will submit to tyranny and oppression". That is not what America is about. Every man and woman must stand up and fight for our rights and freedoms, because the radicals are going to take them away.

Just a side note, is it that my thoughts and opinions are always derogatory towards the democrat party and those that align themselves as such? Yes, for the most part, but not exclusively. The republican party and many of those policitians and folks do at times exhibit disgraceful and shameful conduct as well. People are imperfect, and we all have flaws, and sometimes we do fall short. It's part of being a human creature. But looking at which side seems to cause more stirring and fussing, it's mostly the democrats.

Look at the acts, which cities have the largest problems, those that are democrat controlled. The highest crime, gun violence, etc., are democrat controlled. Who seeks more restrictive laws towards firearms, the democrats. Nearly every issue over restricting rights, freedoms, and liberties, raising taxes, expanding the size and intrusiveness of government, and control, they are democrat initiated. Do the research, check the records, this is true.

Many politicians and groups are calling for more regulations, more intensive background checks, eliminating certain weapons from the marketplace, imposing more taxes on weapons and ammo, and other measures. Now President Trump is in a tough position, because he must do something. There are those who want him to do this or do that, but in the end, he will make up his own mind. Understand that Trump has always been a supporter of the Second Amendment, and for law and order. He has been very supportive, by appointing two originalists Supreme Court Justices, Gorsuch and Kavanaugh. They are strongly supportive of the constitution with a strict interpretation of the law, not wavering over the latest emotional frenzy. President Trump has also appointed almost three hundred federal judges whom also hold a conservative interpretation of the law. Should he be able to appoint yet another good Supreme Court justice, and more judges, then our rights will or should be better enforced.

Some politicians who cry out for more laws and restrictions, like Nancy Pelosi, Speaker of the House, are the ones who have controlled these crime-ridden cesspool inner cities for decades, yet have done nothing to fix them! If the laws they have imposed locally in their own districts have done nothing to stop or even reduce gun violence there, how well will their new proposed restrictions work on the country as a whole? This is a bad direction to fix the problem, it will not work, and real-life data will show how poorly these laws in various cities have done.

Fix the NCIC system. The National Crime Information Center (or NCIC) is a national FBI background check database, developed with guidance from the NRA (National Rifle Association), and is a good system. It is a system that works, if and only if, the law is enforced. Data will show that many states and local areas do Not fully input the data necessary. If it is not in the database, then the background check system does no one any good. Fix it. Make sure all of the necessary data is added, and that is the best solution to the entire background issue.

If you go into a store to purchase a firearm, you will be subject to plenty of screening and background checks. If the system is handled as intended, those seeking firearms the legal way, should keep those purchasers on the "straight and narrow". Criminals don't care about the law, and they will get all the weaponry they desire.

Mental Health and Guns

Mental health is the other key issue along with gun-related violence. Among the leading causes of these people conducting the "mass shootings", is that they are mentally ill. Whether these men (primarily) are just under minor distress or frustration, or total "whack jobs", is irrelevant, they are sick and need help. How to assess a would-be shooter, the signs of mental illness, and then restrict them from obtaining firearms is the heart of the matter. That is very complex. In our free and open society, anything to infringe upon the liberty of personal choice borders on unconstitutional restriction of freedoms. But, laws are suppose to get enacted to protect us. Not to do something, "for the common good of the people", is not an easy option either, There has to be a balance in there somewhere.

Ok, for mental illness laws to work, one needs to define "what" constitutes a mental illness, and, is that grounds for the government to seize your guns? Many states, like California, used to have a strong mental health system. There was a system in place to help people with a wide range of issues, some of which might be valid grounds to keep firearms out of certain patients hands. Under democrat leadership for the last fifteen or twenty years, the mental health system was dismantled. Instead, many mentally ill people are turned out into the streets, and too many seem to get little or no care at all. This is true according to various law enforcement professionals, that statistics on homeless and the level of crime, do correlate. And as California goes, so goes the nation. Many other states have all but scraped their former mental health care, and the homeless problem and crime has increased. Some of these ill folks have used firearms in various crimes, including a few mass shootings, yet are still on the streets. How well will new guns laws work on mentally ill and homeless people?

Now, the mass shootings are the most publicized and politicized events, but the epidemic of gun-related crime in the country is often between individuals or small groups. Gangs, drug-related crimes, domestic violence, and so on, makes up the bulk of gun violent activities. It is no less horrible or tragic, and is also greatly difficult in resolving. Here though, there are laws already established, but need to be enforced. When a person or persons commits a crime (of any type), there are laws that are to be enforced. If the person is found guilty under the due process of certain laws, they are constitutionally banned from possessing or owning firearms. Such cases are those people convicted of felonies, or have been legally pronounced mentally unfit. There are a number of laws and rules relating to such banishment. But the point is, that if the laws are enforced, a great volume of gun-related violence would be stopped. The reality is, the laws are too often not enforced. And the justice system is mired in politics and double-standards.

There are two major areas where the laws should be strengthened and enforced, and they are the NCIC's system and illegal immigration. Both will have a dramatic effect in reducing the gun problem without infringement on our rights.

As mentioned, the NCIC system is a national database that is suppose to be updated (by human input) of those convicted of major crimes, namely felonies. That is a national system, controlled by the FBI, that is suppose to be available to every law enforcement location. Those people seeking a firearm purchase already have to pass a background check, which taps into the NCIC's system. If those people are there, then they are denied the gun purchase. No gun, then less likely a gun-related crime (at least for the law-abiding citizens). The problem is the data is not being input as it should. So a known criminal might be able to get a firearm.

Also a concern is how the justice system turns known violent felons back onto the street too early. Whether via loopholes in the system or politics, some of the most dangerous criminals are allowed their freedom. A large portion of violent and gun related crimes are committed by these known people, and they do not care about gun laws.

Regular and repeat criminals don't usually get their weapons from responsible means, so the NCIC's is less effective in that regard. Still, the system would be helpful in stopping a large portion of known offenders (in the NCIC system) and some mentally ill people from "legally" obtaining guns. The bottom line is that there is no way to stop 100% of gun violence in America, that can not happen.

If America is suppose to be a nation of laws, then that pertains to having a border that limits or prevents unwanted people from entering this country without due process. Our Constitution is very clear about a strong border, with the executive branch, the president, holding certain powers to enforce and protect it. The role of the president is to protect the citizens, and that is exactly what needs to happen at our own borders. No country in the world has an open border and such an influx of people, with no clue who or what these migrants may be. The reality is, that our southern border with Mexico is a mess.

Sadly, half of congress, mostly the democrats, have taken a hostile anti-Trump stance with anything and everything President Trump tries to do. Nancy Pelosi, Speaker of the House, is the worst and most disgraceful anti-American bigot in power. There are many other politicians, including many republicans, that are not serving the people as elected, and have done nothing but exasperated the divide between our peoples. The role of elected leaders is to represent the will and needs of the people, yet all many of these so-called leaders have whined and cried about their own political agendas, in their grab for personal wealth and prominence. And with that, our southern border crisis worsens.

Although America is a nation blended from many nations, coming to this new land seeking a better life, they did so in a controlled and legal manner. Have you ever been to Ellis Island and the Statue of Liberty? Right in the backyard of Manhattan Island, people wanting to emigrate to America were screened and vetted before they were allowed entry. Many were treated for illnesses, and the process was fair and reasonable.

The democrats claim of mistreatment, brutality, and cruel "concentration camp" like conditions preventing emigrants from entering across the south. They have twisted lies and misinformation beyond any reality, and these fake advocates for justice just want to deny President Trump any action to fix the problem. It is all about politics. Filter through the rhetoric, and discern for yourself what is true or valid.

Some of our congressional folks are so disgraceful, citing the Nazi holocaust and the six million Jews that were slaughtered in concentration camps. They are comparing that with conditions of our border. Shame on them, they need to thrown out of office! At least, they need to be taken to places like Auslitz and "learn" what really happened there. These morons are the product of our failed educational system. This subject does relate to our constitutional issues and gun rights, because the school system is and can be used to indoctrinate our children, our future leaders, into believing all sorts of garbage.

In the meantime, thousands of illegals pour across the border nearly unchecked. Those who are caught are then put into comparatively nice living accommodations. They fed, clothed, given lawyers for legal support, then taken to the American heartland, free to enter without the slightest screening. Supposedly, they are to appear in court later to determine their residency status, but few ever show up. Once in the country, they scatter like cockroaches when you turn on the light. And this is all at the taxpayers expense. That is not right or fair to the thousands of would-be emigrants trying to "legally" enter this country, and at their own expense. There is something gravely wrong with this whole border issue, yet the politicians and the media make it a game, a dangerous one at that.

And those who are not caught and detained in the border camps, some are dangerous criminals, carrying guns and drugs. Granted most of the illegal aliens are just seeking a better life, but they have to do so legally. The news media rarely reports on the thousands of cases where illegals are involved in shootings, violent crimes, and so on, but the law enforcement agencies will show the stats otherwise. Mass shootings have happened with some of these "bad hombres", which are real life tragedies. Murders, many involving guns, are too common, which further incites the democrats to take away our guns.

Just like the little story of the sheep and wolf, the politicians would take away our teeth so we will "feel safe". Elections have consequences. You have to vote. You have to encourage others to vote, and get these dangerous and moronic politicians out of office.

Make no mistake, the democrats and some of the weakling republicans are coming for your guns. Constitutional rights or not, we are just an election away from being disarmed.

Learn History

Now on the contrary, good decent law-abiding gun-carrying citizens have stopped thousands of potential crimes, exactly because they were armed. Rarely does the news media relay such stories, it doesn't fit their narrative. In America, it is Our legal and God-given Right to protect our property and ourselves. Our Founding Fathers knew exactly what was needed to be stated and sanctioned in the Constitution to protect the People. An armed citizenry is a safer nation. Guns in the hands of responsible trained average citizens, has done more to protect life and property than all of the legions of police.

As our public school system has made great efforts to minimize and change the teaching of history, our children are not being taught the full story. Our educational system today has all but eliminated the truths and realities of what actually happened in our past, under the guise of political correctness. History happened, and you can not change it, but if you don't teach it (correctly and honestly), history tends to repeat itself. The horrific events that led up to the rise of the Third Reich and World War II can again play out in America. First, make the children ignorant. Teach them about unicorns and sexual preferences. Make them stupid, and they become sheep.

Go back and study history. Go on ebay or Amazon and find yourself a history schoolbook written in the 1980s or earlier. Read what was taught, and compare that with a modern school text. Compare and contrast, and if you could find a history book older than that, how does that differ? Older history books tell of heroic men, with an innovative spirit and hard work, tackling huge challenges, building this country in every aspect of life. Washington, Jefferson, and the other Founding Fathers were heroes, now called racists and other inflammatory falsehoods. These men formed America, and put together what they believed a country of free people should do, and know, to make their young nation strong and prosperous. They had spent years fighting the tyranny of government control, and specifically included a provision for the people to bear arms for their own defense. They knew, that without one's own ability to defend themselves, the government, or another person, would try to control or harm them. Even with other rights and laws in place, power and force has always been the bottom line in protecting personal liberty.

It is therefore so important we, and our children, learn history, true history, the good, bad, and the ugly parts of it. History happened, it's real, but more and more the facts and details are so watered down, the lesson is washed away. If you don't know what happened, how it developed into the myriad of events and outcomes, then you can not learn from the past. If you don't know the past, these events and lessons tend to be repeated.

Does anyone remember Nazi Germany and the Holocaust? Or was that erased from the history books also? Under the guise of law, the socialist controlled government (the National Socialist Party, the Nazi's) made it legal to round up groups of people they disliked, and under "the law", it was legal to kill them. The government sanctioned the murder of their own citizens. Of course, it wasn't called murder; they must have had some legal rationale, which made it acceptable. How many millions of German citizens did their own government murder, by law? Was it 3 million, 6 million? And it was not all people of Jewish heritage; there were Christians and Communists, scholars and professors, and any political opponent the party felt was a threat.

How was that possible? The government took away the guns from private citizens. Confiscation by law, implemented by force, and the people were defenseless to stop it. Is that possible for the United States of America with it's Second Amendment to the Constitution, guaranteeing the Right of the people to own and bear arms? Of yes! It is happening here, and every day, and with every popularized tragedy, full of biased misinformation by the media, groups and politicians are clammering for more gun control laws. Many of these folks are calling for the confiscation of guns by any means.

The Right for a private citizen to own and carry a firearm(s) is greatly threatened, and it is not necessary for the Second Amendment to be ousted off the Constitution. And that includes the stealing of your private property by the government if they confiscate your firearms. Add more laws, more restrictions, more conditions, limited the sale and production of weapons and ammo, just squeeze at the margins.

Long gone are the days when many of the high school kids (boys mostly) had rifle racks and rifles in their pickups. At least at the school I went to. More and more places disallow guns to be carried onto the premise, like government buildings, schools, movie theatres, more retail stores, etc. A "Gun Free Zone" designation by liberal democrat leaders will make us safer? Almost every single mass shooting occurs in gun-free zones. Gun-free zone tells a criminal, "come shoot here, no one will stop you". What about law enforcement? "There is never a cop around when you need one", an old cliche, but too often true. If one were to research and learn the true real-life facts about guns, gun safety, and crime, gun-free zones are death traps, and where citizens are allowed to carry guns, crime is greatly reduced. Guns, in the hands of responsible citizens prevent gun violence, which is factual. Learn for yourself, talk to your local sheriff or police officers, and research the public data.

The Bigger Picture

And actually, at stake is far more nefarious than just another gun law, we are losing our constitutional rights. The bigger picture is the assault of the Rights to Bear Arms, and the Rights of Personal Property Ownership. Certainly, Rights of Free Speech, to Worship freely, the Rights to Assemble, and others are also being stripped away. With each election, each tragedy hyped by the biased "Yellow Journalists", politicians and groups gesture for more laws. This is true and has been happening more and more, and this next election cycle will focus on more controls. It is interesting how the democrats want more control of weapons, new laws and regulations, more taxes to fund ever larger government programs, yet with years and decades of control of the large cities, crime and gun violence continues to increase. These are factual and again do your own research to see for yourself.

How do we, as common individuals, make a difference? Vote. Our best and easiest way to do something of value is to use your voice via our Right to vote. Hopefully, there are candidates worthy to vote for, but the point is this is how change can and does come about in this country. We are a nation of laws, and we have the Constitution that outlines exactly how to make the nation function and the periodic changes in leadership is via the vote. "Use it or lose it", because the democrats have demonstrated over and over again that they want more government, more control over every aspect of daily life, everyone dependent on a government handout or program, with fewer and fewer individual liberties. This again is factual, just look at the latest group of candidates running for office. What do they say, what do they stand for, and what have they done in the past? Do they adhere and support the constitution, or promote bigger government?

By not voting, be complacent because you may be displeased with the candidate choices, the other side is electing their leaders. If you don't vote, the opposing candidates are winning elections, and many of them want to destroy every constitutional right we have. This is fact, look, read, research, and learn for yourselves what is happening.

And who are being elected. Those gaining political and legal power (to make laws that govern our lives) has been going to liberals, progressives, socialists, and dishonest deceptive politicians, seeking power and riches, and in absolute contradiction to our established liberties and freedoms. Many of these folks are democrats, although to be fair, not all democrats adhere to the new party platform. Many republicans and other politicians may be vile snakes as well. There are poor leaders in that are republicans and independents as well. Please don't misunderstand that! Overall, the New Democrat Party is a very different party than what existed before. And because these people are gaining office, they are making laws, some are very bad laws.

Thieves, Liars, and Hypocrites

Some of these ideas and thoughts are repeated over and over. That is done purposefully, because they are important to hear. My hope is that you glean some thought provoking questions, and that you will seek to learn more, and do more.

The tragedy of America, in all its splendor and glorious "free and open" society, is that a few "bad apples" take advantage of the "goodness" that America was founded upon. This country was founded on the cornerstone of Christian-Judeo principles of doing good and right to others, to allow them the freedom of personal choice and the opportunity to rise above, and make their lives better. This is done without the heavy hand of rulers dictating every aspect of life, or with cruel oppression.

In this country, public officials take an oath of office to abide and uphold the statutes of the constitution, and their very basic requirement. It is a promise to work for the good will of the people that elected them freely. Yet in such openness, it is too easy for power, greed, and corruption to turn everything good and right about America, into the tyranny is suppose to suppress.

What are today's biggest social issues? The democrats (and some republicans) say it is crime, gun violence, poverty, and drugs, especially in the larger inner city areas. These leaders cry out for tolerance, fairness, better schools, and so on, but what is the reality? Look at every major city or problem area, and see who is in charge. The majority of these areas are controlled by democrats, many whom have been in power for decades.

In real life, look at people like Nancy Pelosi, who controls San Francisco, I was there years ago, used to ride the trolley cars, eat on the wharf, and drive all through the city. It was almost like a magical theme park. For the past decades of her control, the city has become a disgusting sewer of drugs, hoards of homeless people, crime, and human waste everywhere. Yet Nancy safe and sound in her high walled tower and armed guards, has become wealthy at the citizens expense. She and her cronies, bilk ever increasing taxes from businesses and the common worker, controls the media, and screams for more gun laws and controls.

It is the same with the city of Baltimore under Cummings, Chicago under Ron Enamanuel, Bill deBlasio controlling New York, and so and on and so on. These places are a mess! The rulers have become rich kings, catering to the wealthy desirable areas under their rule, yet neglect the poor neighborhoods, which are war zones. Here also, they clamor for more taxes and regulations, control of crime and gun violence, yet they use the propaganda of the media to retain power. Every city, every "hotspot" of crime and problem, these elected hypocrites have used power and the taxpayers purse to fatten themselves, to the suffering of the people. Shame on them!

These wealthy elitist politicians control the media, with support of wealthy patrons, so decades of control benefit the few, at the expense of the masses. And who are the ones most abused and neglected? Often it is the African-American and Hispanics, for whom these leaders claim to support. No, they are no more than slaveholders, like the democrat leadership of old.

Shame on these politicians. They took an oath of office to the electorate, stewards of the public trust, yet they have abused their positions, and regulate away their liberties. And what do they want to do with gun laws? How well would these leaders implement new regulations?

The Grand Strategy

It is said by some, that there is a Grand Strategy, not just to take away our rights to bear arms, but all of our rights and freedoms. As you listen to the media, the elitists, leftist leaning politicians, movie stars, many college professors, and whacko's of every other sort, seeking a new utopia, equality and fairness, and everything for free, they reveal the plot. There are a more publicly vocal group seeking socialistic ideals, which is contrary to everything America is based upon.

The grand plan is destroy America. We nearly saw it come about under the Obama leadership, where strife and division was the excuse for more controls and regulations. It is a real life push to turn America in a socialist country, controlled by a few powerful players. And as all socialist countries go, the turn to communism (totalitarianism) soon follows. In the process, rights, freedoms, and liberties become fewer and more restricted, and then eventually made null and void. Guns and the Second Amendment stand in the way.

Remember the Revolutionary War? Not much of it, it's roots, or but a few of the details, are taught in school anymore. Now it is viewed as "racist" or "unfair", so keeping with the doctrine of "dumbing our children down", such topics are merely a mention. Our forefathers fought for the freedom from tyranny (the English King at that time) that controlled every part of daily life. It was the rebellion, regular citizens armed with guns that made it possible. Now as the politicians are tightening the noose on our rights of self-defense and freedom from a tyrannical central government, history is poised to repeat itself again.

Most striking during the Obama years was how he (and others, like the media) divided the people. We were staunchly united after 9-11, but he used race and income to divide us into smaller groups, pitting one against the other. It was black against white, brown against white, poor versus the rich, the evil big corporations against the poor, and so on. Divide and conquer.

 The strategy is very clear, first divide the unity of the people. Use the media to misinform and as propaganda to spread distrust and discord. Change the educational system to make the next generation "dumb", dependent on government, and stifle individualism. Teach evolution, sexual preferences, tolerance for everything except God, and the fantasy of a unicorn utopia. Teach everything except the characteristics of our forefathers, hard work, independence, perseverance, and faith. Our children are confused, no idealism, no incentive to be innovative or become leaders, or to build. Want to take over a country? Brainwash the children.

Then take God out of the public sphere. America and western civilization is founded on Biblical truth. But get rid of the dependence on God, our moral compass, and the people will be lost and scattered like sheep, looking to themselves, and moral relativism to discern right from wrong. "Everything is acceptable, with no consequences or condemnation, just be tolerant". Sound familiar?

Next, take away the guns. Without a counter force, the private ownership and Right to defend yourself, then the tyranny of government will take control. History has shown us over and over, that this is true.

With the people divided, our prodigy dumb and aimless, disarmed, then all you need is a "crisis". With a crisis, such as "climate change", the people will turn to a strong leader with all of the answers to fix everything, and solve all of the ills of society. And with that America is destroyed. Again, does anybody remember the rise of Nazi Germany, and their savior, Adolph Hitler?

Our guns are the tools to protect all of the rights and freedoms we are guaranteed by our founding document. We, as the people, need to act. We need to learn for ourselves what is happening, relearn history, contact our leaders and politicians and help them understand our concerns. We need to vote, and encourage others to vote as well. We need to arm ourselves, train, and perhaps join like-minded organizations. And certainly, we all need to get our knees and pray for wisdom and guidance from Almighty God.

What about Abortion?

The media and the leftist elites that push for gun control, are the same ones that enact laws to kill babies. Yes, abortion is not part of the gun issue per se, but there are some interesting parallels.

On the one hand these people call for help for illegal alien children at the border, but turn around and enact laws to kill our own citizens. Yes, there is an epidemic of gun-related deaths, but what about abortion? If a criminal with a gun attacks you, and you do not have one, then you become an innocent victim. What about a baby, the most precious and innocent of all life, then murdered in cold blood, under the guise of legality? Which is worse, or what's the difference? In America, you have the Constitutional Right to defend yourself, even with a gun. Who defends a baby?

The latest New York State abortion law, essentially sanctions death to their citizens. Human babies can be killed late in the pregnancy, even after the baby is born and takes its first breaths. Up until now, every statue in this country would call that murder! Not so anymore. This is a violation of our Rights of Worship, Speech, and the pursuit of happiness, and other guarantees as laid out in the constitution. Other states like Vermont and Virginia has wanted similar laws. The deceptive politicians and legal establishment will profess the contrary, but they are vicious liars and murderers in their own right. We are a nation of laws, and the rule of law is the intent of how the government is suppose to be govern our society. But laws are made that are not always good or right for the people. All abortion laws are legal, but none of them are right. It is by the twisting and perversion of right and wrong by filthy lawyers and crooked politicians that has brought us to this point. It is time to act and do something.

The majority of these politicians are democrats. Look at the voting records, it is very telling. These are the same hypocrites that cry out about the injustices of handling illegal alien children being held by border control officers. But when it comes to killing human babies, of our own citizens, they and the media remain silent.

Do you think these elected officials care about your gun rights? Do you think they are upholding the statutes of the constitution? Whatever issue you are talking about, gun laws, rights of life, illegals crossing into our country, what is happening is the shredding of the foundational principles and protections laid out in the constitution. The more they create new laws, the closer America will become like Nazi Germany, Soviet Russia, or China. Each of these evil regimes killed millions and millions of their own citizens, with no one to stop them.

And what about a child's "the right to life"? The abortion question, is not just a freedom of religious worship, but it is also a freedom of speech. Perhaps the greater overall question is whether it is right and lawful for the government to kill, or sanction the killing, of its own citizens. Although the Supreme Court allowed the ability to kill unborn babies as a rule of law in Roe vs. Wade, is it right? No, it is a disgusting and abhorrence to everything good and honorable that this country touts to be. Murder is murder. An unborn child is still a human being, up until now. How can these wise lawyers in the Supreme Court, who are charged in upholding the constitution, allow such debauchery? Because liberal presidents and politicians appointed liberal-thinking justices into the court, with the results of bad laws getting enacted. They care nothing about the Rule of Constitutional Law, but instead focus on the emotional political fad of the day. America is heading down the road to destruction if this trend continues.

When the State of New York and Vermont have passed new laws allowing the death of babies, the voting assembly members applauded the new laws with resounding glee! It is said that liberty will die with resounding applause. Soon, more states will enact laws contrary to tradition and justice. That is sounding more like Nazi Germany. Are we really there? Whether life begins at conception or when a baby draws its first breath is irrelevant. The question is how can we as a nation allow the murder of our own innocent and defenseless citizens? We are suppose to be a nation ruled by law, but not all laws are good or just. Where is the sanity of our lawmakers? This is murder, plain and simple.

Elections have consequences. You vote for good people to lead us that defend life and liberty, or not. We have seen the definitions of right or wrong changed to suit the desires of elected officials. You vote for your hearts desire, and apparently it's for death. And to have such leaders in power, they will continue to enact laws that will subvert and limit our rights.

 Now if this horrid lust of killing innocent life is not overruled, then the rights of free speech, religious worship, and "the pursuit of happiness", are made mute. Our freedoms as guaranteed under the

US Constitution are destroyed. Those lawmakers, supporters of such legislation, and any group or organizations that adheres with such, are murders and co-conspirators. Then the ideas of truth and justice in America is just a lie!

What follows next? Well, because the murder of babies is made legal, the next step is to broaden that "definition" of whom can be (legally) murdered. Next will be young children no longer wanted by their parents, or perhaps the elderly will be killed at the whim of the court. Then from there, any opposition group or segment of citizens, like white males, Christians, deplorable Trump supporters, and so on, can face the death squads (by law). "When the sword is unsheathed, it is difficult to put it back without first spilling blood."

Here also, if and when the government is allowed to restrict your rights to own firearms, or takes them away completely, then there will be no more questions about religion, free speech, abortion, rights to assemble, protests against the government, and so on. The Second Amendment is the Second one for a reason, it's important. The right of the citizens to defend themselves against a government that goes crazy is vitally important. It is the private ownership of firearms by the common people that protects the freedoms and liberties guaranteed in the Constitution. Without our Right to Bear Arms, how can we defend against tyranny?

Go back and study recent history. Not on the internet, or from a school textbook after 1980, they are full of false and distorting information. The older the history book, the more honest it was written. You can find them in old book stores, yard sales, and even on ebay or Amazon.

"Those who gain power will abuse it, and then they will oppress the people, which then they will start murdering the citizenry." Strongly ponder these thoughts.

And What to Do?

America is at a crossroad; it's a time of strife and division among two major lines of thinking. One side is trying to uphold and live by the traditional values and framework of the country, namely the Constitution. The other side is trying to tear down every positive thing in America because "it's unfair", "racist", "full of greedy rich white men", "the republicans don't care about the planet", and every other nonsense imaginable. They are the ones that are pushing for a government all-powerful solution to solve all the nations ills, more control, "equality and fairness for all", confiscate the guns, and everyone will live happily in a unicorn-filled safe la-la land. As Nancy Pelosi, Speaker of the House, irrationally screams, "why does anyone need more than one gun? The answer is simply, "because of socialist nut-jobs like her".

Buy more guns, stock up on ammo, train, and join like-minded organizations that support your values. Vote. Vote, and encourage everyone you meet to vote as well. Your vote is your voice, the correct way to make the peaceful change in leadership. Also, learn, research the topics of the day and decide for yourself, which is true, and what is biased agenda-driven rhetoric. Study our history, and make sure your children or grandkids learn our true history as well.

More About Losing Our Liberties

Is it possible to lose our Constitutional rights and freedoms? These are guaranteed under the law, aren't they? Yes, but no.

With each election, it results in more radical thinking politicians taking office, by which they get laws and regulations passed to restrict our gun ownership, for instance.

Similarly with the rights of worship, there are increasing limits on what can and can not be publicly done (or seen). Not so long ago, one could pray in school. The Ten Commandments were posted in every courtroom and on most public buildings. Christmas and the name of Jesus were commonplace during the Christmas Holiday season.

Now, by laws and restrictions, it takes lawyers and legal battles to be able to meet on a public campus to have a time of prayer. How about courthouses are being stripped of the Ten Commandments, for which our laws are based upon. There are groups that make all sorts of ludicrous claims; but they just want anything Christian removed. How about last Christmas? How many battles did these atheists groups and organizations demanding the end of Christ-mas related everything fight all over the country? There are news stories where anti-Christian groups would set up satanic emblems and decorations next to Nativity scenes.

These are all attacks on our constitutional rights of free worship. Apparently to many of these groups, everything is tolerated except Christianity, or anything that invokes the name of Jesus. These are the same groups that preach tolerance and free speech, acceptance of other viewpoints, transparency, except Christ.

Our freedom of speech, part of that 1st Amendment Right, along with Religion, is also greatly under attack. There more and more laws that restrict what you can say against another person or group. Some of these are "Hate Laws" that also have consequences for speaking adversely. This silencing of open discussion, debate, or defiance, is control of our of free speech, basically censorship.

Among the recent rhetoric of censorship has to do with the Black Lives Matter and Antifa terrorist gangs. Right now, there is a lot of division and tension being promoted by the media and leftist democrats, to glorify these rioting mobs, while defaming and suppressing any support for law enforcement or the rule of law. It has been verified that employees in certain companies have been fired and reprimanded for speaking against the BLM movement. Politicians, and just about anyone, is afraid of speaking or acting against them for fears of retaliation, assault, or violence. The BLM and Antifa are free to terrorize, destroy property, intimidate officials, and worse, with no consequences from "authority". To speak against them, brings all sorts of condemnation. This is censorship. It's true, watch the news.

Some politicians seek more control over us by enacting more laws and regulations in every area of our lives. What if you spoke against a government agency or a governmental employee? Laws are being passed to limit what you can say against the government. What was accountability of government by the people, laws are starting to restrict that opposition, else face serious consequences. Learn who the candidates are before you vote. Does the party platform, their set of ideals, align with your own? How do you want to live? Our country is founded on some simple absolute Rights; free speech and freedom to worship are the 1st Rights in the Constitution for a reason. It's important.

What about the Freedom of religious worship? Our Judeo-Christian roots that bore this country and our entire legal system have been greatly under attack. We are free to worship whom and what we like, or nothing at all, without the interference of government mandating what we can do.

The idea of "separation of Church and State", has been grossly portrayed by those seeking to abolish Christianity in America. Thomas Jefferson and Hamilton had written about this matter from the beginning, citing that "not separation from government, but rather that "government shall not impose a religion". In other words, government would not declare a State religion. Being a person of faith, whatever you believe, and part of the government structure, should not be an issue. It is, and watching every Supreme Court nomination hearing, and even most Cabinet level screenings, there are those people, mostly the democrats, that scream about the separation of Church and State. Having a person that holds a belief and moral compass in public office is a good thing. Look at some of the corrupt lying filthy politicians currently serving in office, and then decide which is better.

If democrat politicians (who have the mission to control the lives of the people) are elected, they will enact more laws to reduce or eliminate the rights and privileges we hold. That is pure fact, check the laws proposed and their voting records.

As we lose our freedom of speech (again as an example), we become slaves to the government. And what happens if there is no accountability? Dictatorship. No freedoms, the government becomes all-powerful, no opposition, and they hold the sole power of life and death over every citizen. Study human history, it's scary.

Don't the republicans seek control also? Yes, sure they do, as all that are elected are subject to the lusts of power and control. It's just that in recent times, the democrat party has become so radical in their quest to control people by restrictive laws and regulations, they have become totally nuts. Is that right or even fair? Some think it's fine, others are less happy, but the movement towards a socialist and totalitarian slavery will end all of the liberties and freedoms we still have.

This trend in our elections and the types of people elected to office is actually frightening. Too many are pushing for a government led controlled society, socialism. Recent polls of college students suggest that about half favor socialistic ideals. Do our kids even know what they are talking about? No, because history and civics are not taught truthfully in the public school system or at the collegiate level. Then, how can they answer such questions? All countries that have embraced that style of "slavery" are unproductive, with a people that are unhappy. Why do you think illegal immigration is at an all-time high? Those nations embracing government control, historically, have not remained very long.

Other Freedoms to Lose

Our gun rights, is not the only right and freedom we can lose, but all of the others as well.

The Right to bear arms is one part, but the Rights of Private Property ownership are greatly threatened too. The Second Amendment protects the citizens' right to bear arms, for personal and family protection, but also to stand against tyrannical rulers. This fight has escalated in recent years, flamed by the biased media, and outspoken elitists. Here too, the critics claim that having guns is unsafe, yet those individuals have armed security and walled homes. More common than ever before, is the talk about gun confiscation, "Red Flag" laws are and will become common, where "the government" can barge into your home and seize your guns.

And for the government to seize your property without due process, they are violating the 4th, 5th, and 6th Amendments, among others. It is all about the laws and rules we are to be governed by, and there are those that want to strip them away. But if there is a law (like a Red Flag law ina particular state), does that make it okay or right? Laws are written by those we elect to office. Know who the candidates are, and what they propose, because elections have consequences that can be ruinous for our nation.

Without the Right to defend yourself, do you think the rights of speech or worship will remain for long? Once the people are disarmed, then the government will become vicious. Study history. Again, recall the rise of Nazi Germany, the communist take over of Russia, Chairman Mao, Paul Pott, and others. No guns, equals no resistance.

We have plenty of good Gun laws in effect, but not adhered to in most states. Rather than add new laws to restrict gun ownership, how about enforce the current laws? For example, the background check laws for gun purchasing was developed with the assistance of the NRA. The way it is supposed to work is that criminal offenders are suppose to have their names and information submitted by the state and local levels into the NCIC database. From there, those with access to the system can then approve or deny a purchase via the information submitted. Therein lies the rub, information has to be added into the system, which is done at the state or and local levels. Not to do so, makes the whole background checking system incomplete due to the lack of relevant data. It is a good law and a good system, if it were used as intended.

Also, beware the "Red Hat" laws. As hinted to earlier, they are unconstitutional, at least if implemented by the federal government. Many states are implementing what is called Red Hat laws, whereby any person can simply accuse another person of being "dangerous".

This then triggers law enforcement to confiscate that accused persons' firearms. Based merely on hearsay, without proof, and without due process. Is that not a violation of many of our personal rights and freedoms? Yes, and it is yet another way the leftists are starting to "void" the Second Amendment.

As you look at the history of every nation that has turned socialist, the final thing the government would do is to remove the guns. Remove the ability of the citizens to fight against injustice, and the people will be easily controlled. Remove the guns, and all other rights and freedoms can not be defended. Again, take Nazi Germany for example. There was strong active opposition to the rise of the socialists, but once the guns were seized, the Nazis eliminated all of the critics. And we are talking about the government killing its own citizens. It is that scary.

How about the Rights to Assemble, Freedom to speak out against the government, worship, due process, and more? Could meeting at church be met with armed police or death squads? Not yet in America, but many places around the world, yes! Christian persecution is literally a life or death struggle in many countries. That can happen here too! Elect leaders hostile to the Christian faith, and watch what happens. Previously, there was a law that the preacher could not talk about politics or governmental actions in the pulpit. To do so, was to invite possible arrest. That has been removed, thanks to President Trump, so the truth and politics can be talked about openly. That can change back as easily.

The Health Care Issue

Although not a right or freedom per se, it is a topic that strongly relates to electing leaders who make laws that impacts all of us. Some politicians and others claim that health care is a Right. Constitutionally, it is not.

Look what happened with the Affordable Care Act (Obama Care), or the laws revolving around abortion. Were they good laws imposed by the politicians? These same people are the ones seeking to create ever more restrictive gun laws. How well do you think that will turn out?

As far as health care laws, women's rights groups, Planned Parenthood, many politicians, and socialist elites are trying to push their agendas as part of the health care issue. Many of the ideas they want to see enacted into federal law are just crazy. Women have different needs than men, that is biological fact, and should not include the fluid gender dysphoria popularized by the left. Yet many of these groups and individuals are pushing for surgery coverage for gender changes, gender surgery changing on small children, and other mandates, that would be forced upon us via taxation. That infringes on our Rights of free speech, religious liberty, due process, fair taxation, and probably other areas.

No disrespect intended for those who want to live their lives differently than others, that is your Liberty to be a unique and untethered person. Be anything you want to be, that's fine, but when laws are enacted to "force" or "mandate" one group's agenda over all the people, that is unconstitutional.

Again, look at Obamacare, the Supreme Court finally overturned the mandate that forced penalties for non-conforming to the law. They enforced the law through taxation, a favorite trick to force a people into submission. Without the change of government to the Trump leadership, Obamacare and all of its total waste and poor design would have become entrenched forever. Obamacare did not work, plain and simple, and forced everyone to conform to an unconstitutional law.

The Health Care issue has become a national focal point, perhaps rightly so, but the manner of which many politicians force legislation down our throats restricts our freedoms. This is a State issue, where the states themselves should create the laws that effects their own citizens. But the power of the states has been greatly forfeited to the federal level, always lured in by federal tax dollars. Here too, gun laws are a State issue, not a federal infringement.

Abortion (or the murder of our citizens) is not greatly apart from the gun issue. It is exactly about constitutional rights, and how the Supreme Court ultimately defines the matter. As the Court is divided in basic interpretation philosophy, popular fad of the day versus originalism, our freedoms and liberties can be further infringed upon.

Women are women, and have special medical needs and concerns that men can not fully comprehend. By God's design, women are the ones that bear life. By politics and the laws of insanity, those groups, like Planned Parenthood, say that a woman even giving birth, should have the say whether to murder the baby. They argue about rights, a woman's right to choose, and all sorts of ludicrous arguments. And the laws are such that the doctor, and supposedly doctors, then determines the life or death outcome. Are such procedures allowed under the various health insurance programs? Do you know how much of your tax dollars are funding procedures like this? Is that right or fair?

What about private insurance plans versus taxpayer funded public programs like medi-care? Do I have the say where and how my tax dollars can or should be used for health care coverage? Again, it's about voting and electing leaders to design laws to allow or deny various medical procedures, forced upon the majority trough taxation. It is about money, power, and control, who has it, and who is trying to get it. The victims are the women, children, and society as a whole.

The socialist medical programs enacted by Obama were not only unconstitutional, but it promoted abortion, and other immoral practices. The one-payer system, that Obama Care was trying to implement, was that government would control it, and therefore becoming a crucial part of our lives. It took tax dollars from every person, to pay for things like abortion, which is wealth redistribution, and contrary to conscience of unwilling citizens. It was a terrible and costly debacle, infringing on our rights of religious worship and beliefs, and enforced by government imposed penalties and the overtly powerful IRS. Do you understand what socialism is? It is government control; all decisions are made under the thumb of a handful of leaders, without regard to individual rights, freedoms, or liberties.

Now do you think these same political guru's that pushed for this health care debacle would handle new gun laws any better? They lied to us! Every now and then, the media plays that video clip from that key presidential debate in 2012, where Obama says, "you can keep you doctor, and everyone will save about $2500 on their costs". Liars, and deceiving charlatans, never trust these politicians. These are both democrat and republicans that do this, not just one party.

The Party "Not" for the People, or Life

The new democrat party promotes an "open door" stance in regards to borders and immigration, government oversight of religious values, control of education, a government sponsored health care system, highly restrictive gun ownership (if not outright confiscation), and a crackdown on freedom of expression. They encourage government programs to take care of every need, including income equality. They elevate the status of illegal immigrants, including the criminals and child-slavery bondsmen, over legal and natural American citizens. Life of the unborn has no rights, and therefore can be slaughtered almost at a whim. The new party promises higher wages via the redistribution of wealth, taxing the evil rich (white) aristocracy. Is this what people want from their governing bodies?

The radical wing uses slogans and bold words to promote their beliefs. "Be tolerant of other people and their lifestyles." "Save the planet by ending fossil fuels." "The government is your family, your provider, and your god." The bottom line is, they want a government controlled Socialist State. The decisions and policies for the people, made by an elite group of "honorable intelligent" leaders, as they know best how to govern the nation. They promise the "good life", without the worry of consequence. Research and learn for yourself, who and what the new democrat party really stands for, but they do not stand up for American or Christian values.

Wake up Brethren. Wake up America. This is happening. Over the past several decades or so, we have seen so many traditions and what we would call Christian values being eroded. Look at marriage for instance. In the 1940s and 50s, divorce was not very common. Now, at least half of all people have been divorced at least once! Socialistic teachings, human-centered, sensitivity (or tolerance) training, are forces seeking to sway voters into this "progressive thinking". Anything to take the focus off of Christianity, and put it on world values, have eroded every traditional norm. The erosion of everything American is very real, and about to sink this nation. Many pastors say, "we are one generation away from losing Christianity in this country. It's true, look at church attendance. Most are nearly empty, and the few that attend, are mostly older folks. Youth, there are some, but not many. Sports and entertainment venues are packed, but the churches are empty and closing.

It is also said that the end of American liberty is just one election away. Perhaps the next one, we will see what type of fools the people have elected, and what they will do to the constitution. Total erosion of this country's' foundation is real.

What Type of Leaders?

Who we elect, will result in laws by lawmakers, like those in New York, Vermont, and Virginia. The 2018 mid-term elections were wrought with manipulation and deceit, with the backing of main stream media, and powerful wealthy donors. The democrats were using Gestapo-like tactics to quell any resistance, twisting the truths and news, and used the "mob" to intimidate and harass opposition. Fake ballots turned election results to democrat in a number of races, and voter fraud, via mail-in ballots was rampant. "Democrats can't win elections without cheating", has a lot of substance.

This is not the Democratic Party of JFK or even Bill Clinton. What was the welfare of the working man under the Kennedy era Democrats, which was the cornerstone of the party, has given way to radical socialistic doctrine, with legions of brain-washed stooges to carry out mob violence and endless protests. Rather than come up with solutions to fix an issue, or to make lives better for the people, they use rhetoric and hate speech, and the double standard to advance a dark agenda. That had in fact prompted the newly elected house legislatures in New York, Vermont, and Virginia, to design and passes such horrid abortion laws.

Hey, as noted, elections have consequences, and if people don't get out there to vote, this is what happens. And what about your guns? Gone. They are coming for your private property, that is a fact.

Again, as an example, President Trump and the border wall. The will of the people that elected Trump, want a border wall and increased national security. It is factual that large amounts of drugs, crime, slavery, and masses of invading people, come across the southern border, half of which is in Texas. Most Americans want this invasion to end. America is a sovereign nation that has the right to have a border, and restrict people and activities from entering the country. This is also factual, and mandated in the US Constitution that the president has the right and authority to protect and enforce our national borders from outside influences.

Bill Clinton argued and demanded a wall for protection along the border. So did Obama. Pelosi, Schumer, Ms. Clinton, and many other democrats, as shown on numerous video clips. Each cited the needs for border walls and security. Yet, because Trump is so greatly hated by most of the democrat leadership, the media, and their brainwashed zombies, they all now oppose border security. For President Trump to succeed on this key election issue, the democrats would suffer greatly. Therefore, despite protecting Americans, our rights, our safety, they will oppose the wall until the next election day.

On and on, there seems to be examples of prominent party leaders that profess one thing, yet do the opposite. Too many of them make promises, only to deny such upon gaining office. Granted, politics is an ugly business sometimes, and some candidates and elected people are morally corrupt, but that seems to be normal in this day and time in which we live.

The latest opinion polls suggests that President Trump has an approval rating of about 40 to 65%, and Congress about 12 to 14%. Whether accurate or not, the fact is that many people don't trust or like our elected leaders. Then vote them out. Learn about the candidates before they get into office, and join with those that are like-minded. Use your rights and freedoms to assemble, speak up, and then vote.

A Couple Final Thoughts

If democrat politicians (who have the mission to control the lives of the people) are elected, they will enact laws to reduce or eliminate the rights and privileges we hold. In particular, our rights to bear arms, the freedom to worship God as we like, the ability speak in opposition of the government or laws that are enacted, our rights to join together in public or private, are all gravely at risk. As we lose our freedom of speech (again as an example), we become slaves to the government. Power and control unchecked, will destroy a nation. Killing the most innocent and precious of God's creation, our babies, He will repay in kind, and destroy this nation. God will not be mocked, even if cleverly worded by a legal document.

Don't the republicans seek control also? Yes, sure they do, as are all elected officials are subject to the lusts of power and control. More and more republicans cave into the whims of democrat leadership, being weaklings without principles. It is just that in recent decades, the democrat party has become so radical in their quest to control people through restrictive laws and regulations. Is that right or even fair? Some think it's fine, others are less happy, but the movement towards a socialist and totalitarian slavery will end all of the liberties and freedoms we still have.

This trend in our elections and the types of people elected to office is actually very scary. Too many candidates, elitists, organizations, and segments of the population are pushing for a government-led, governmental-controlled society. Free health care, free schooling, abortion on demand, all have great costs. Nothing is free. It comes from high taxation rates of the working man, but also through the limitations imposed on our freedoms to make personal individual choices and decisions.

Our system of government was designed and set up to assure the people would have the liberty to become all they can aspire to do (if not murdered at birth). The freedom of free and open speech, and religious liberties, have been the cornerstone of this country, rooted in the process of free and open elections. Every vote counts, and every citizen has a duty to make this country better, according to their own conscience.

As our society writhes with turmoil of the legality of guns and life, the next election cycle approaches. Many groups are seeking to undermine our rights and liberties to vote, to own and carry firearms, to have free and open speech, our rights to worship, and the rights afforded to life. It is critical for the survival of the nation as a whole; to learn about the candidates and what they value, and stand with those who think the same. This is no time for professing Christians, or any American to sit idle, there is just too much at stake.

As mentioned in the beginning, this little story is critically important to keep in mind. "A bunch of sheep were happily grazing in the field, enjoying the comforts of their lives. A wolf came out of the woods and killed one of the sheep. In a panic, they formed a consensus on what to do. They decided the best way to keep themselves safe was to remove all of their teeth. Later, the wolf came back and killed them all." Set that clearly in your mind. Laws only work if they are enforced, and, if everyone follows them. Those who are unlawful, and there are too many in America, do not follow the laws. Be wary of the politicians.

And lastly, keep in mind what Gods word tells us, repent; turn away from what we are doing. There are many scriptures that continually repeat this, like from Zechariah 1:3 and 4, in part reads, "...Thus says the Lord of hosts, 'Return to Me' declares the Lord of Hosts." "...Return now from your evil ways and from your evil deeds". Not to do so, invites the wrath that is coming to this country. May the Lord be with you, and all of us.

The Amendments to the United States Constitution

It is nice to have an easy reference source for all 27 of the amendments. Read them, learn them, and then listen to the media and see how many are mentioned, and cited correctly.

Bill of Rights (Amendments #1 to 10)

Amendment I

Congress shall make no law respecting an establishment of religion, or prohibiting the free exercise thereof; or abridging the freedom of speech, or of the press; or the right of the people peaceably to assemble, and to petition the Government for a redress of grievances.

Amendment 2

A well regulated Militia, being necessary to the security of a free State, the right of the people to keep and bear Arms, shall not be infringed.

Amendment 3

No Soldier shall, in time of peace be quartered in any house, without the consent of the Owner, nor in time of war, but in a manner to be prescribed by law.

Amendment 4

The right of the people to be secure in their persons, houses, papers, and effects, against unreasonable searches and seizures, shall not be violated, and no Warrants shall issue, but upon probable cause, supported by Oath or affirmation, and particularly describing the place to be searched, and the persons or things to be seized.

Amendment 5

No person shall be held to answer for a capital, or otherwise infamous crime, unless on a presentment or indictment of a Grand Jury, except in cases arising in the land or naval forces, or in the Militia, when in actual service in time of War or public danger; nor shall any person be subject for the same offence to be twice put in jeopardy of life or limb; nor shall be compelled in any criminal case to be a witness against himself, nor be deprived of life, liberty, or property, without due process of law; nor shall private property be taken for public use, without just compensation.

Amendment 6

In all criminal prosecutions, the accused shall enjoy the right to a speedy and public trial, by an impartial jury of the State and district wherein the crime shall have been committed, which district shall have been previously ascertained by law, and to be informed of the nature and cause of the accusation; to be confronted with the witnesses against him; to have compulsory process for obtaining witnesses in his favor, and to have the Assistance of Counsel for his defense.

Amendment 7

In Suits at common law, where the value in controversy shall exceed twenty dollars, the right of trial by jury shall be preserved, and no fact tried by a jury, shall be otherwise re-examined in any Court of the United States, than according to the rules of the common law.

Amendment 8

Excessive bail shall not be required, nor excessive fines imposed, nor cruel and unusual punishments inflicted.

Amendment 9

The enumeration in the Constitution, of certain rights, shall not be construed to deny or disparage others retained by the people.

Amendment 10

The powers not delegated to the United States by the Constitution, nor prohibited by it to the States, are reserved to the States respectively, or to the people.

Additional Amendments (#11 to 27)

Amendment 11

The Judicial power of the United States shall not be construed to extend to any suit in law or equity, commenced or prosecuted against one of the United States by Citizens of another State, or by Citizens or Subjects of any Foreign State.

Amendment 12

The Electors shall meet in their respective states and vote by ballot for President and Vice-President, one of whom, at least, shall not be an inhabitant of the same state with themselves; they shall name in their ballots the person voted for as President, and in distinct ballots the person voted for as Vice-President, and they shall make distinct lists of all persons voted for as President, and of all persons voted for as Vice-President, and of the number of votes for each, which lists they shall sign and certify, and transmit sealed to the seat of the government of the United States, directed to the President of the

Senate;-The President of the Senate shall, in the presence of the Senate and House of Representatives, open all the certificates and the votes shall then be counted;-The person having the greatest Number of votes for President, shall be the President, if such number be a majority of the whole number of Electors appointed; and if no person have such majority, then from the persons having the highest numbers not exceeding three on the list of those voted for as President, the House of Representatives shall choose immediately, by ballot, the President. But in choosing the President, the votes shall be taken by states, the representation from each state having one vote; a quorum for this purpose shall consist of a member or members from two-thirds of the states, and a majority of all the states shall be necessary to a choice. And if the House of Representatives shall not choose a President whenever the right of choice shall devolve upon them, before the fourth day of March next following, then the Vice-President shall act as President, as in the case of the death or other constitutional disability of the President-The person having the greatest number of votes as VicePresident, shall be the Vice-President, if such number be a majority of the whole number of Electors appointed, and if no person have a majority, then from the two highest numbers on the list, the Senate shall choose the Vice-President; a quorum for the purpose shall consist of two-thirds of the whole number of Senators, and a majority of the whole number shall be necessary to a choice. But no person constitutionally ineligible to the office of President shall be eligible to that of Vice-President of the United States.

Amendment 13
Section 1

Neither slavery nor involuntary servitude, except as a punishment for crime whereof the party shall have been duly convicted, shall exist within the United States, or any place subject to their jurisdiction.
Section 2

Congress shall have power to enforce this article by appropriate legislation.

Amendment 14
Section 1

All persons born or naturalized in the United States and subject to the jurisdiction thereof, are citizens of the United States and of the State wherein they reside. No State shall make or enforce any law which shall abridge the privileges or immunities of citizens of the United States; nor shall any State deprive any person of life, liberty, or property, without due process of law; nor deny to any person within its jurisdiction the equal protection of the laws.

Section 2

Representatives shall be apportioned among the several States according to their respective numbers, counting the whole number of persons in each State, excluding Indians not taxed. But when the right to vote at any election for the choice of electors for President and Vice President of the United States, Representatives in Congress, the Executive and Judicial officers of a State, or the members of the Legislature thereof, is denied to any of the male inhabitants of such State, being twenty-one years of age, and citizens of the United States, or in any way abridged, except for participation in rebellion, or other crime, the basis of representation therein shall be reduced in the proportion which the number of such male citizens shall bear to the whole number of male citizens twenty-one years of age in such State.

Section 3

No person shall be a Senator or Representative in Congress, or elector of President and Vice President, or hold any office, civil or military, under the United States, or under any State, who, having previously taken an oath, as a member of Congress, or as an officer of the United States, or as a member of any State legislature, or as an executive or judicial officer of any State, to support the Constitution of the United States, shall have engaged in insurrection or rebellion against the same, or given aid or comfort to the enemies thereof. But Congress may by a vote of two-thirds of each House, remove such disability.

Section 4

The validity of the public debt of the United States, authorized by law, including debts incurred for payment of pensions and bounties for services in suppressing insurrection or rebellion, shall not be questioned. But neither the United States nor any State shall assume or pay any debt or obligation incurred in aid of insurrection or rebellion against the United States, or any claim for the loss or emancipation of any slave; but all such debts, obligations and claims shall be held illegal and void.

Section 5

The Congress shall have power to enforce, by appropriate legislation, the provisions of this article.

Amendment 15
Section 1

The right of citizens of the United States to vote shall not be denied or abridged by the United States or by any State on account of race, color, or previous condition of servitude.

Section 2

The Congress shall have power to enforce this article by appropriate legislation.

Amendment 16

The Congress shall have power to lay and collect taxes on incomes, from whatever source derived, without apportionment among the several States, and without regard to any census or enumeration.

Amendment 17

The Senate of the United States shall be composed of two Senators from each State, elected by the people thereof, for six years; and each Senator shall have one vote. The electors in each State shall have the qualifications requisite for electors of the most numerous branch of the State legislatures.

When vacancies happen in the representation of any State in the Senate, the executive authority of such State shall issue writs of election to fill such vacancies: Provided, That the legislature of any State may empower the executive thereof to make temporary appointments until the people fill the vacancies by election as the legislature may direct.

This amendment shall not be so construed as to affect the election or term of any Senator chosen before it becomes valid as part of the Constitution.

Amendment 18
Section 1

After one year from the ratification of this article the manufacture, sale, or transportation of intoxicating liquors within, the importation thereof into, or the exportation thereof from the United States and all territory subject to the jurisdiction thereof for beverage purposes is hereby prohibited.

Section 2

The Congress and the several States shall have concurrent power to enforce this article by appropriate legislation.

Section 3

This article shall be inoperative unless it shall have been ratified as an amendment to the Constitution by the legislatures of the several States, as provided in the Constitution, within seven years from the date of the submission hereof to the States by the Congress.

Amendment 19

The right of citizens of the United States to vote shall not be denied or abridged by the United States or by any State on account of sex.

Congress shall have power to enforce this article by appropriate legislation.

Amendment 20
Section 1

The terms of the President and Vice President shall end at noon on the 20th day of January, and the terms of Senators and Representatives at noon on the 3d day of January, of the years in which such terms would have ended if this article had not been ratified; and the terms of their successors shall then begin.

Section 2

The Congress shall assemble at least once in every year, and such meeting shall begin at noon on the 3d day of January, unless they shall by law appoint a different day.

Section 3

If, at the time fixed for the beginning of the term of the President, the President elect shall have died, the Vice President elect shall become President. If a President shall not have been chosen before the time fixed for the beginning of his term, or if the President elect shall have failed to qualify, then the Vice President elect shall act as President until a President shall have qualified; and the Congress may by law provide for the case wherein neither a President elect nor a Vice President elect shall have qualified, declaring who shall then act as President, or the manner in which one who is to act shall be selected, and such person shall act accordingly until a President or

Vice President shall have qualified.

Section 4

The Congress may by law provide for the case of the death of any of the persons from whom the House of Representatives may choose a President whenever the right of choice shall have devolved upon them, and for the case of the death of any of the persons from whom the Senate may choose a Vice President whenever the right of choice shall have devolved upon them.

Section 5

Sections 1 and 2 shall take effect on the 15th day of October following the ratification of this article.

Section 6

This article shall be inoperative unless it shall have been ratified as an amendment to the Constitution by the legislatures of three-fourths of the several States within seven years from the date of its submission.

Amendment 21
Section 1

The eighteenth article of amendment to the Constitution of the United States is hereby repealed.

Section 2

The transportation or importation into any State, Territory, or possession of the United States for delivery or use therein of intoxicating liquors, in violation of the laws thereof, is hereby prohibited.

Section 3

This article shall be inoperative unless it shall have been ratified as an amendment to the Constitution by conventions in the several States, as provided in the Constitution, within seven years from the date of the submission hereof to the States by the Congress.

Amendment 22
Section 1

No person shall be elected to the office of the President more than twice, and no person who has held the office of President, or acted as President, for more than two years of a term to which some other person was elected President shall be elected to the office of the President more than once. But this Article shall not apply to any person holding the office of President, when this Article was proposed by the Congress, and shall not prevent any person who may be holding the office of President, or acting as President, during the term within which this Article becomes operative from holding the office of President or acting as President during the remainder of such term.

Section 2

This article shall be inoperative unless it shall have been ratified as an amendment to the Constitution by the legislatures of three-fourths of the several States within seven years from the date of its submission to the States by the Congress.

Amendment 23
Section 1

The District constituting the seat of Government of the United States shall appoint in such manner as the Congress may direct:

A number of electors of President and Vice President equal to the whole number of Senators and Representatives in Congress to which the District would be entitled if it were a State, but in no event more than the least populous State; they shall be in addition to those appointed by the States, but they shall be considered, for the purposes of the election of President and Vice President, to be electors appointed by a State; and they shall meet in the District and perform such duties as provided by the twelfth article of amendment.

Section 2

The Congress shall have power to enforce this article by appropriate legislation.

Amendment 24
Section 1

The right of citizens of the United States to vote in any primary or other election for President or Vice President for electors for President or Vice President, or for Senator or Representative in Congress, shall not be denied or abridged by the United States or any State by reason of failure to pay any poll tax or other tax.

Section 2

The Congress shall have power to enforce this article by appropriate legislation.

Amendment 25
Section 1

In case of the removal of the President from office or of his death or resignation, the Vice President shall become President.
Section 2

Whenever there is a vacancy in the office of the Vice President, the President shall nominate a Vice President who shall take office upon confirmation by a majority vote of both Houses of Congress.

Section 3

Whenever the President transmits to the President pro tempore of the Senate and the Speaker of the House of Representatives his written declaration that he is unable to discharge the powers and duties of his office, and until he transmits to them a written declaration to the contrary, such powers and duties shall be discharged by the Vice President as Acting President.
Section 4

Whenever the Vice President and a majority of either the principal officers of the executive departments or of such other body as Congress may by law provide, transmit to the President pro tempore of the Senate and the Speaker of the House of Representatives their written declaration that the President is unable to discharge the powers and duties of his office, the Vice President shall immediately assume the powers and duties of the office as Acting President.

Thereafter, when the President transmits to the President pro tempore of the Senate and the Speaker of the House of Representatives his written declaration that no inability exists, he shall resume the powers and duties of his office unless the Vice President and a majority of either the principal officers of the executive department or of such other body as Congress may by law provide, transmit within four days to the President pro tempore of the Senate and the Speaker of the House of Representatives their written declaration that the President is unable to discharge the powers and duties of his office. Thereupon Congress shall decide the issue, assembling within forty-eight hours for that purpose if not in session. If the Congress, within twenty-one days after receipt of the latter written declaration, or, if Congress is not in session, within twenty-one days after Congress is required to assemble, determines by two-thirds vote of both Houses that the President is unable to discharge the powers and duties of his office, the Vice President shall continue to discharge the same as Acting President; otherwise, the President shall resume the powers and duties of his office.

Amendment 26
Section 1

The right of citizens of the United States, who are eighteen years of age or older, to vote shall not be denied or abridged by the United States or by any State on account of age.

Section 2

The Congress shall have power to enforce this article by appropriate legislation.

Amendment 27

No law varying the compensation for the services of the Senators and Representatives shall take effect, until an election of Representatives shall have intervened.

With all of this mentioned and discussed, my hope is that you will learn more, vote and encourage everyone to vote, and enjoy the many great and wonderful liberties we have in this country.

About the Author

I grew up in a middle class family, had a father that worked, a mother that stayed home and raised children, the typical traditional American home. We had a small house, one car, (no) white picket fence, we had pets, guns, regular schooling, church-goers, watched news and various TV shows, hunted and shot targets, and had all of the cliche normal things in life typified during the 1950s and 60s. Life was normal and decent, reasonably peaceful, and safe.

My father was a veteran, worked a blue collar job, and was a straight-line democrat, just like his father before him. The Kennedy era thinking of party politics was pretty much his thinking as well. And for many decades, that seemed to work well in America. I too learned and adopted similar ideas of how life and government should work and coexist.

But that has changed radically over the past couple decades, as the democrat party is no longer the party of the average working man. One would best describe the party as what we used to call the Communist-Socialist party during that earlier era. Now the party is all about hate speech, bigotry, division, dirty-politics, rampant dishonesty and deception by party leaders and candidates, and everything revolving around government control. This is no longer the democrat party America once loved.

The candidates and false narratives they promoted were enough to make me switch to the Republican Party. Over the last many election cycles while the democrats drove further left, I pushed my family and friends to switch parties and vote further right. Not that the republicans are perfect by any means, but they do hold to more of the values and principles I do. The biggest area where they align with my own thinking are the ideas of limited government, the sanctity of life, and support for the Constitution. Upholding our rights and freedoms are more their forte, so this is where we will stay.

My hope is to share these thoughts with you, so that you can glean some insight of the struggle we face over our dying liberties. Thank you reading this.

Also consider these other books written about our Rights and Freedoms. These also are found on Amazon Kindle under the Politics section. Look for:

"The Democrat Blue Wave is the Zombie Apocalypse"

by T. H. Logwood
ASIN: B07MYBFKT1

* * * * *

The American Civil War II
By T. H. Logwood
ASIN: B08CQ4PDMQ.

* * * * *

"The End of American Liberty"
by T. H. Logwood
ASIN: B07HPYZWTF

* * * * *

"The Democrat Blue Wave is the Texas 2nd Alamo"
by T. H. Logwood
ASIN: B07N7N2WG6

* * * * *

"The End of American Freedom"
by T. H. Logwood
ASIN: B07MSJ4QD7

* * * * *

"The U.S.S. La Porte (APA 151), The Pearl of the Pacific"
by T. H. Logwood
ASIN: B07L6JXRB9

* * * * *

"A Walk in the Sub-Alpine Meadows: A Look at the Tuoloume
Meadows Ecosystem"
by T. H. Logwood
ASIN: B07HM928TH

* * * * *

"Collecting Old Stock Certificates: A Look at the Past"
by T. H. Logwood
ASIN: B07HNX1FGK

www.ingramcontent.com/pod-product-compliance
Lightning Source LLC
Chambersburg PA
CBHW051235250726
48655CB00006B/2782